# A Dorling Kindersley Book
Conceived, edited and designed by DK Direct Limited

## Note to parents

**What's Inside? Planes** is designed to help young children understand the workings of planes, from the turn of the century to the present day. It shows what was inside an early airship, how a jumbo jet can carry hundreds of people speedily round the world, and how flying in a microlight might feel like hanging from a kite. It is a book for you and your child to read and talk about together, and to enjoy.

**Editor** Hilary Hockman
**Designers** Juliette Norsworthy and Helen Spencer
**Typographic Designer** Nigel Coath

**Illustrators** Ray Hutchins/Linden Artists,
Icon Design Solutions, Chris Lyon,
Jon Sayer, Brian Watson/Linden Artists
**Photographers** Mike Jerram (cover and page 6),
Gary Kevin, Matthew Ward
**Written by** Alexandra Parsons
**Consultants** Andrew Nahum and Kelvin Wilson
**Design Director** Ed Day
**Editorial Director** Jonathan Reed

First published in Great Britain in 1992
by Dorling Kindersley Limited,
9 Henrietta Street, London WC2E 8PS

A CIP catalogue record for this book is available from the British Library.

ISBN 0-86318-983-0

Printed in Italy

# WHAT'S INSIDE?
# PLANES

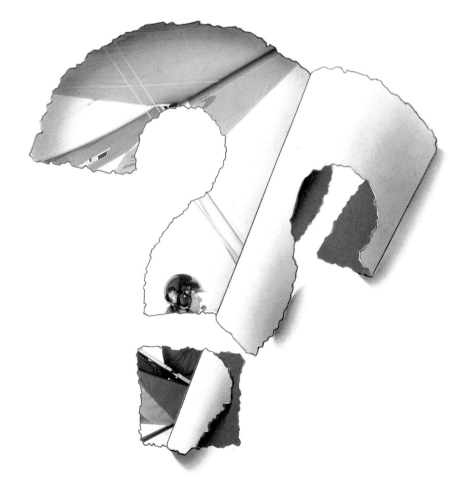

## DORLING KINDERSLEY
### LONDON • NEW YORK • STUTTGART

# AIRSHIP

Airships stay in the air because they are full of a special gas to keep them up. Today, airships float about in the sky with big advertisements on the side. Sixty years ago they carried passengers, which was fine as long as the people weren't in a hurry. Airships could only cruise along as fast as a slow car.

These moveable panels at the back were used to steer the airship, like a rudder steers a boat.

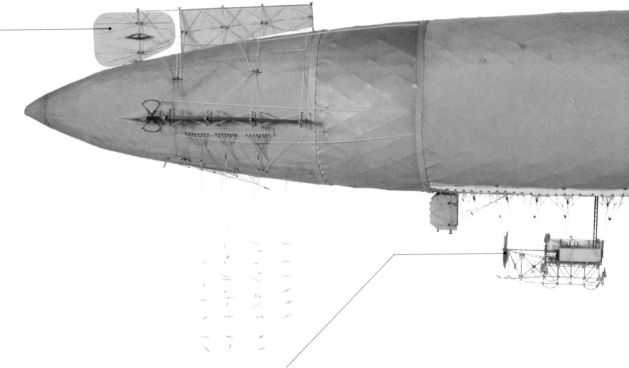

Each car or gondola hanging underneath the airship had an engine. The engines turned the propellers and kept the airship moving forwards.

The gas in an airship is lighter than air, just like the gas in party balloons that will float up and away unless you hold on tight.

The airship had to be as lightweight as possible. It was covered with cotton material.

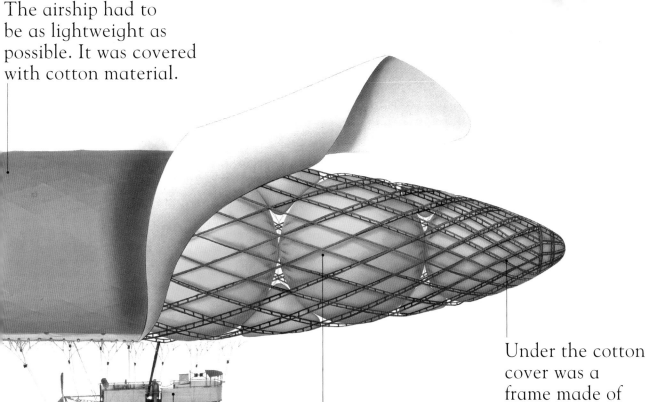

Under the cotton cover was a frame made of criss-cross wooden trellis.

Inside the frame were 15 gas balloons.

Passengers and crew were carried in this gondola.

When flying overland, the pilot used a map to find out where they were travelling. He just leaned over the edge of the gondola and followed roads and rivers.

# EARLY PLANE

The body of this plane is made of wood, fabric, wires and glue!
It's hard to believe it now, but somehow, nearly 100 years ago,
a Frenchman called Louis Blériot flew this flimsy little craft
$23\frac{1}{2}$ miles across the English Channel.

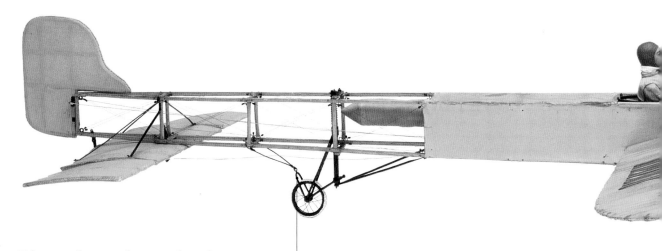

Blériot knew how wheels were
attached to bicycles. He copied this
idea to join the wheels to his plane.

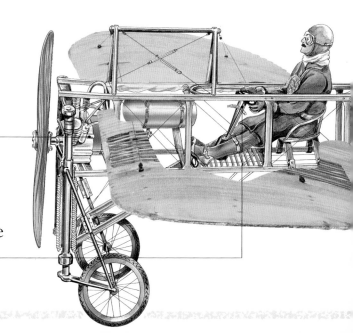

The engine turned a big
wooden propeller and this
moved the plane forwards.

The pilot controlled the plane from
the cockpit. From here he could move
the wires that steered the plane.

Once this plane had made a successful flight, everyone wanted one! Blériot set up a factory and made 100 just the same.

The wings kept the plane up in the sky, supported by the wind rushing past.

The material covering the wings was shrunk tight onto the framework and sealed with a special glue.

The rudder steered the plane. It was moved by wires that ran from the controls in the cockpit to the tail.

The frame was made of a strong, bendy type of wood and was kept in place by wires.

# LIGHT AIRCRAFT

If you've ever been to an airshow, you'll almost certainly have seen a tiny Pitts Special like this in the air. It's for daredevil stunts such as looping the loop. It flies upside down so often that its top and underside are painted in different colours so the people on the ground can see which way up it is!

The wings and tail are covered in material to keep the plane light. This is just like Blériot's cross-Channel plane nearly 100 years ago.

The main body of a plane is called the fuselage.

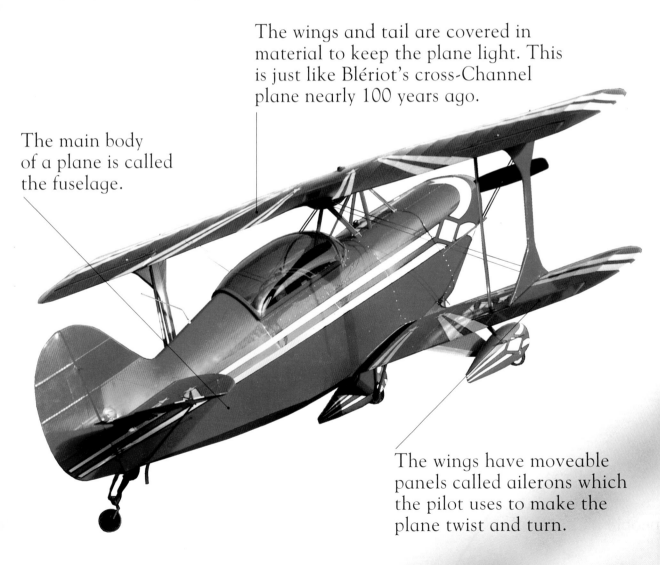

The wings have moveable panels called ailerons which the pilot uses to make the plane twist and turn.

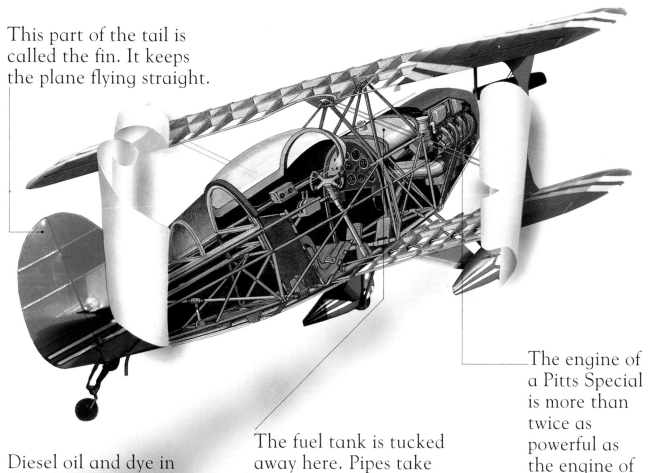

This part of the tail is called the fin. It keeps the plane flying straight.

The engine of a Pitts Special is more than twice as powerful as the engine of a family car.

The fuel tank is tucked away here. Pipes take the fuel to the engine.

Diesel oil and dye in the exhaust pipes make the coloured smoke that comes out during an airshow.

This is a pretty spectacular trick. It's called wing-walking.

Lots of Pitts Specials are built at home by people using kits.

# FLYING BOAT

In the days before modern jets, air travel was a luxurious and leisurely business. Planes had to stop quite often to take on supplies and fuel. Airports cost a lot of money to build and there weren't many of them, so planes were built that could land on water.

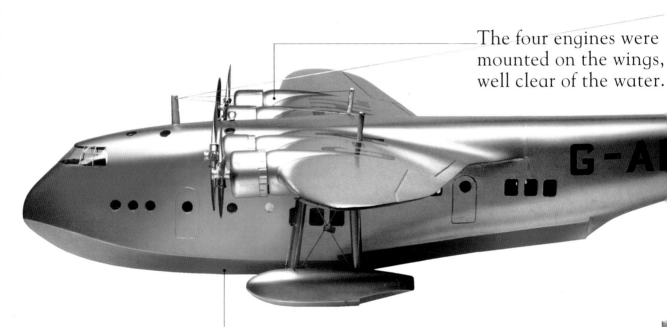

The four engines were mounted on the wings, well clear of the water.

The underside of a flying boat is called the hull. Not surprisingly, it was shaped like the bottom of a boat.

The captain and the radio operator sat here, in the cockpit.

On some flights, passengers didn't have to sleep in their seats. The plane would stop for the night and they were taken to a luxury hotel nearby.

This is the lounge with tables, comfortable chairs and vases of fresh flowers.

Freshly cooked meals were prepared in a proper kitchen by a chef.

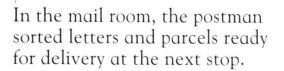

In the mail room, the postman sorted letters and parcels ready for delivery at the next stop.

# HELICOPTER

This helicopter is an air-ambulance. Helicopters can land and take off from just about anywhere, so an air-ambulance can rescue people from the most awkward places, like the top of a mountain or a life raft bobbing about in the sea. It can rush an injured person off to hospital within minutes.

There is a little rotor on the tail. If it wasn't there, the helicopter would just spin round and round like a top.

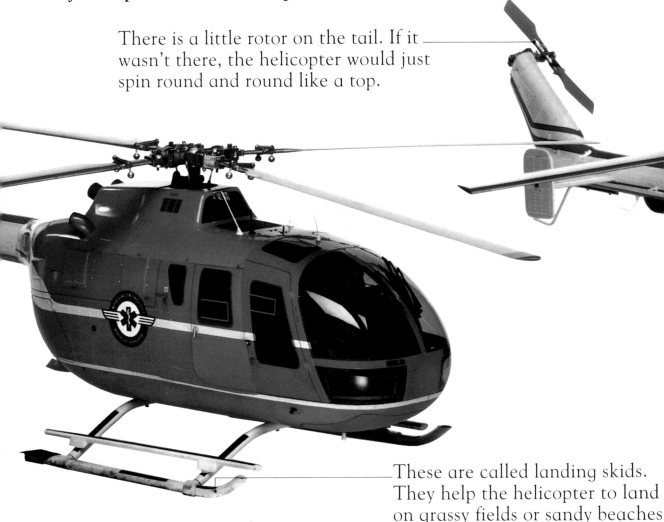

These are called landing skids. They help the helicopter to land on grassy fields or sandy beaches as well as on proper helipads.

The letter H painted on top of the lighthouse makes it easier for the helicopter pilot to see where to land.

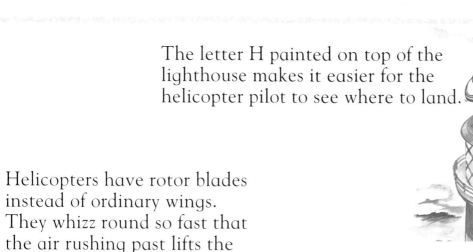

Helicopters have rotor blades instead of ordinary wings. They whizz round so fast that the air rushing past lifts the helicopter into the sky.

The engine is powerful and uses up fuel very quickly. Helicopters can't stay in the air for long without coming down to refuel.

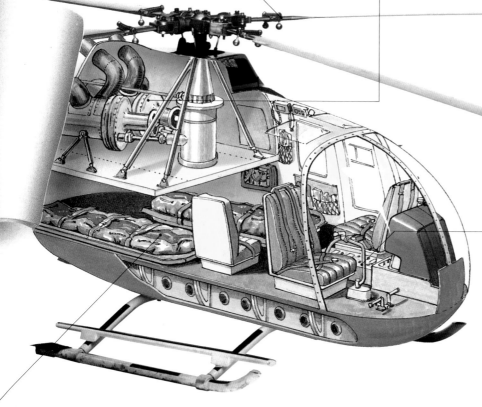

Flying a helicopter is tricky. There are so many controls to think about at the same time, that it's a bit like trying to pat your head while you're rubbing your tummy.

Like any ambulance, this air-ambulance is well equipped with life-saving equipment.

# JUMBO JET

Modern jets are criss-crossing the world all the time, taking
people from place to place as quickly and efficiently as possible.
The jumbo jet is one of the biggest aeroplanes ever made.
It can carry over 500 people.

Food is prepared in kitchens
on the ground, then heated
up in the galleys on board.

Children are well looked after on planes.
The cabin crew give them games and
crayons while the grown-ups watch a
film or listen to music on headphones.

There's an upstairs
and a downstairs
on a jumbo jet.

Passengers' cases are
put in cargo holds.

Seats are fixed to the floor. They
tip back so passengers can rest.
Babies travel in special cots.

All aboard! Tickets please! Modern jets provide transport almost like your local bus service.

There are no propellers on a jet. The engines move the plane forwards by sucking in air at the front and pushing it out at the back.

Jets fly high above the clouds where the air is very cold and where you can't breathe. The plane is completely sealed so the windows don't open.

# FIGHTER PLANE

Fighter planes like this F16 have to move quickly and easily so they can sneak up on the enemy and get out of the way fast if danger strikes. Some modern jet fighters can even fly backwards. They can climb high or dive low, skimming the tops of trees.

A fighter plane can have its fuel topped up while it's flying along.

The pilot sits in an ejector seat. If he is about to crash, he pulls a lever and...whoosh! The canopy flies off, his seat shoots out, and a parachute opens.

The pilot sits tilted back to stop him fainting if he has to change direction fast.

The nose-cone contains the instruments for guiding weapons and for finding out where other planes are.

This is where air rushes into the jet engine right in the middle of the plane. A fighter plane is like a huge engine with wings and weapons.

14

The pilot has to be able to see all round him in case an enemy plane comes up from behind. The canopy over the cockpit is made of very strong clear plastic.

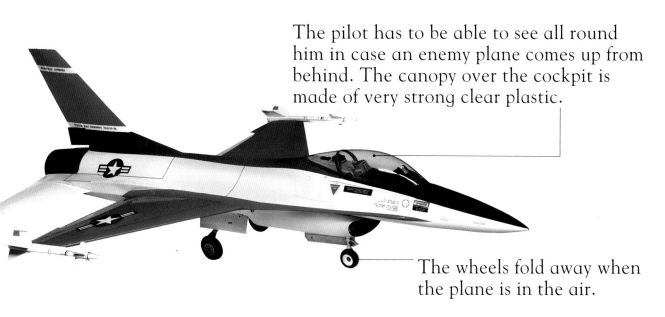

The wheels fold away when the plane is in the air.

The F16 carries wing-tip missiles. It can also carry heavy bombs and guns under the wings.

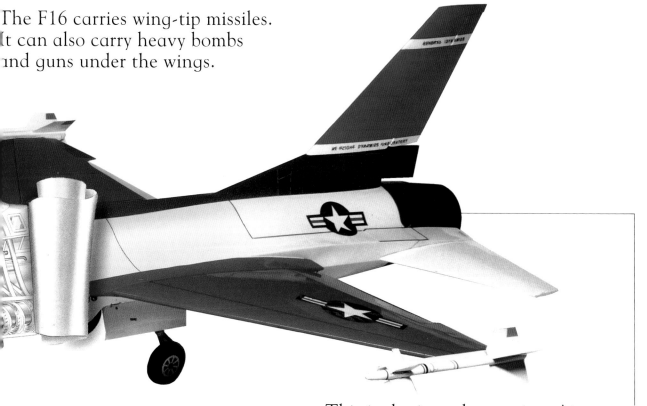

This is the jet exhaust pipe. Air comes out here, pushing the plane along.

# MICROLIGHT

A microlight is like a huge kite powered by a little engine. You can travel at about 50 miles an hour and up to 20,000 feet high in one of these. People fly them for fun, but in Africa they are being used to spot illegal hunters of elephants and rhinos.

The wing is made of material held in shape by aluminium tubes called ribs.

The cockpit is made of fibreglass, a strong but light plastic.

The engine drives the propeller.

This is the engine. The very first microlight was made from a hang glider and a chainsaw engine!

Haven't you ever wished you could climb on a kite and fly above the tree tops? That's what flying in a microlight feels like.

The pilot pulls the control bar back to fly faster and pushes it forwards to slow down.

The instruments tell the pilot how fast and how high the microlight is flying.

The seat belts hold the pilot and passenger safely in their seats.

The passenger sits here, behind the pilot. They both wear crash helmets and warm clothing.

This is the throttle pedal, like you would find in a car. The pilot uses it to rev up the engine for take-off and to climb high in the air.